BLS WORKING PAPERS

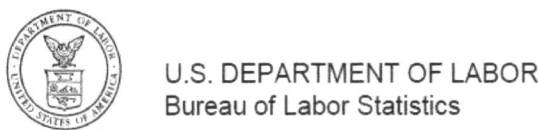

U.S. DEPARTMENT OF LABOR
Bureau of Labor Statistics

OFFICE OF PRICES AND LIVING
CONDITIONS

Modeling Consumer Demand for a Large Set of Quality Differentiated Goods:
Estimation and Welfare Results from a Systems Approach

Roger H. von Haefen, U.S. Bureau of Labor Statistics
Daniel J. Phaneuf, North Carolina State University
George R. Parsons, University of Delaware

Working Paper 353
February 2002

Modeling Consumer Demand for a Large Set of Quality Differentiated Goods: Estimation and Welfare Results from a Systems Approach[*]

Roger H. von Haefen
Bureau of Labor Statistics

Daniel J. Phaneuf
North Carolina State University

George R. Parsons
University of Delaware

COMMENTS WELCOME

January 15, 2002

[*]We thank Kerry Smith, Matt Massey, and seminar participants at North Carolina State University and the Environmental Protection Agency (EPA) for comments and suggestions. All remaining errors are our own. Phaneuf acknowledges financial support from the EPA through contract #R826615010, and Parsons acknowledges financial support from the National Oceanic and Atmospheric Administration (NOAA) through a Delaware Sea Grant. The views expressed in this paper are the authors alone and in no way represent the views of the EPA, NOAA, or BLS. Corresponding author: Daniel Phaneuf, Department of Agricultural and Resource Economics, NCSU, Box 8109, Raleigh, NC 27695.

Modeling Consumer Demand for a Large Set of Quality Differentiated Goods: Estimation and
Welfare Results from a Systems Approach

Abstract

We develop an approach for estimating individual level preferences for a large set of quality

differentiated goods and for constructing Hicksian welfare measures for price and quality

changes within the demand system framework. Our approach uses a simulated maximum

likelihood estimation procedure for recovering estimates of the structural parameters and an

adaptive Metropolis-Hastings algorithm for constructing Hicksian consumer surplus estimates.

We illustrate our approach with a recreation data set consisting of day trips to 62 Mid-Atlantic

beaches.

JEL Classification: C15, D12, D61, Q26

1. Introduction

In this paper we develop a demand system approach for estimating preferences for an arbitrarily large set of quality differentiated goods at the individual or household level. We apply the model to an outdoor recreation data set consisting of day trips to 62 beaches in the Mid-Atlantic region and analyze the welfare effects of changes in beach characteristics and availability. Interest in the value of beach recreation opportunities arises from policy makers' need to assess the merits of beach nourishment programs and to measure the damages resulting from acute environmental accidents that impact beach availability. The Hicksian consumer surplus estimates reported in this paper address these issues and represent the first welfare measures derived from a theoretically consistent demand system model that accounts for interior and corner solutions and accommodates a large set of quality differentiated goods.

Because of the computational difficulties associated with estimating and generating welfare measures from demand system models, nearly all empirical strategies for modeling consumer choice for many goods have relied on the discrete choice random utility model (RUM) developed by McFadden [1974]. A large and growing body of empirical research has shown that the discrete choice RUM framework is attractive for modeling extensive margin choices made on single choice occasions, but how the framework can be modified or augmented to represent consumer choices made over longer time horizons when realized demands are a mixture of interior and corner solutions remains an unresolved modeling issue. At present, there are several discrete choice RUM-based approaches for modeling consumer choices in these situations (e.g., Morey, Rowe, and Watson [1993] Hausman, Leonard, and McFadden [1995], Feather, Hellerstein and Tomasi [1995], Parsons and Kealy [1995]), all of which have strengths and weaknesses. Some common features of these RUM-based modeling strategies are the assumptions that the time horizon of choice can be decomposed into separable choice occasions,

3

that the objects of choice on each choice occasion are quality-adjusted perfect substitutes, and, with rare exception, that income effects are absent.[1] In part because of the restrictiveness of these assumptions, Phaneuf, Kling, and Herriges [2000] (hereafter PKH) and Phaneuf [1999] have recently suggested modeling consumer choice in these situations within a unified demand system framework that consistently accounts for interior and corner solutions. Their empirical applications, however, consider only a small number of quality differentiated goods, and thus the relevance of the demand system framework for policy applications with many goods remained uncertain.

We demonstrate in this paper that if preferences are additively separable the demand system framework can be estimated and used to generate Hicksian welfare measures for applications with many goods. Additive separability implies strong restrictions for consumer behavior, but in our view these restrictions have close analogs to the assumptions embedded in the discrete choice RUM models that have traditionally been used for this class of problems. Moreover, the demand system framework has the advantage of combining the extensive and intensive margins of consumer choice for all quality differentiated goods in a coordinated and behaviorally consistent framework.

In addition to permitting the construction of welfare measures for a large set of quality differentiated goods, our empirical models incorporate several innovations over existing demand system recreation applications. Our specifications allow a subset of the parameters entering the direct utility function to vary randomly across individuals in the population and employ a simulated maximum likelihood estimation procedure. From an econometric perspective, introducing random parameters is attractive because it facilitates a relatively flexible specification for the unobserved heterogeneity without substantially expanding the number of estimable parameters. In addition, our empirical application incorporates an approach to welfare

4

measurement suggested by von Haefen [forthcoming] that conditions on an individual's observed choice. In contrast to traditional approaches to welfare measurement from RUM models (e.g. Small and Rosen [1981]), we construct welfare measures in this paper by simulating the unobserved heterogeneity entering preferences such that our model predicts observed behavior perfectly at baseline conditions. The structure of the model is then used to predict how individuals respond to price, quality, and income changes. To implement our conditional approach, we develop a sequential Monte Carlo procedure that employs an adaptive Metropolis-Hastings algorithm. Although conditioning on an individual's observed choice adds more complexity to our welfare calculation procedure, it substantially reduces the number of simulations necessary to generate precise welfare estimates as well as the computational time involved.

Using an unusually rich data set consisting of 540 Delaware residents' beach recreation activities, our empirical application examines the demand for day trips to 62 ocean beaches in the Mid-Atlantic region. Due to infrequent but acute oil and toxic spills, state officials in New Jersey, Delaware, Maryland, and Virginia occasionally close beaches for health and safety reasons. In addition, beach erosion caused by rising sea levels, development, and natural causes has led state officials to initiate beach nourishment programs throughout the region. Since beach recreators are among the individuals most impacted by beach closures and erosion, our welfare scenarios can inform state officials of the potential economic losses arising from these impacts.

The remaining structure of the paper is as follows. The next section gives a general overview of the issues involved in demand system estimation and welfare calculation with large choice sets. Section 3 follows with a discussion of the empirical specifications and estimation strategies we employ in this paper, and Section 4 discusses our strategy for construction welfare measures. Section 5 discusses the Mid-Atlantic beach recreation data set we use in our application, and Section 6 summarizes our estimation results. Section 7 discusses our welfare scenarios and results, and Section 8 concludes.

2. General Overview

In principle, there are two generic strategies for developing demand system models that consistently account for both interior and corner solutions and can be applied to problems with many goods. The first, referred to as the Kuhn-Tucker approach by Wales and Woodland [1983], exploits the Kuhn-Tucker conditions that implicitly define the consumer's optimal consumption bundle. Alternatively, Lee and Pitt [1986] develop a demand system framework that relies on the concepts of notional demand and virtual price functions (Neary and Roberts [1980]). Although these approaches are dual, we focus on the Kuhn-Tucker framework in this section and in our subsequent empirical work. Much of our general discussion that follows, however, transfers to the dual approach in a straightforward manner.

As discussed in Wales in Woodland and PKH, the Kuhn-Tucker framework begins with a specification of consumer preferences represented by a continuously differentiable, strictly increasing, strictly quasi-concave direct utility function, $U(x, Q, z, \beta, \varepsilon)$, where x is an M-dimension vector of consumption levels of the quality differentiated goods that are consumed in non-negative quantities, Q denotes an $M \times K$ matrix of commodity specific quality attributes of the goods in x (i.e., $Q = [q_1 ... q_M]^\mathsf{T}$ where q_k is a $K \times 1$ vector of attributes for site k), z is an essential Hicksian composite commodity representing spending on all other goods, β is a vector of structural parameters entering preferences, and ε is a vector or matrix of unobserved heterogeneity. Because ε is interpreted as components of the utility function known to the individual but unobserved and random from the analyst's perspective, the structure of preferences is consistent with McFadden's random utility hypothesis (see McFadden [2001] for a recent discussion).

6

The consumer maximizes utility subject to a linear budget constraint and M non-negativity constraints:

$$\max_{x,z} U(\boldsymbol{x},\boldsymbol{Q},z,\boldsymbol{\beta},\boldsymbol{\varepsilon}) \quad s.t. \quad \boldsymbol{x} \geq 0, \quad \boldsymbol{p}^{\mathsf{T}}\boldsymbol{x} + z = y, \tag{1}$$

where $\boldsymbol{p}$ is an M-dimension vector of prices, y is income, and the price of the Hicksian composite commodity is normalized to one with no loss in generality. In addition to the constraints in (1), the Kuhn-Tucker conditions that implicitly define the optimal solution to the consumer's problem can be written:

$$\partial U / \partial x_j \leq (\partial U / \partial z) p_j, \quad j = 1,...,M. \tag{2}$$

Estimation of the structural parameters entering the preference specification within the Kuhn-Tucker framework exploits these weak inequalities. Equation (2) and an individual's observed choices place restrictions on the support of the distribution of the unobserved heterogeneity. Assuming the errors representing unobserved heterogeneity are drawn from some known family of distributions with parameter vector Σ, these restrictions permit recovery of estimates for $\boldsymbol{\beta}$ and Σ within the maximum likelihood framework.

From an econometric perspective, the Kuhn-Tucker model can be interpreted as an endogenous regime switching model where regimes are defined as combinations of interior and corner solutions for the M goods and determined by equation (2). When dealing with applications involving large sets of quality differentiated goods, two related issues must be addressed in estimation. The analyst must choose a flexible yet parsimoniously parameterized direct utility function. This requires restricting the dimension of $\boldsymbol{\beta}$ to be sufficiently low. Moreover, the analyst must specify a distribution for the unobserved heterogeneity that has an estimable parameter vector Σ that is of relatively low dimension and that allows calculation of the multiple dimensional integrals that correspond to the probabilities of observing each of the

2^M possible regimes. If these issues are adequately addressed, the Kuhn-Tucker framework represents a viable approach to modeling consumer choice for many quality differentiated goods in a systems framework.

Welfare measurement from demand system models raises a separate and in many ways more complicated set of issues. The Hicksian consumer surplus CS^H associated with a price and quality change from (p^0, Q^0) to (p^1, Q^1) is implicitly defined as:

$$\max_{\omega \in \Omega} V_\omega(p^0, Q^0, y, \beta, \varepsilon) = \max_{\omega \in \Omega} V_\omega(p^1, Q^1, y - CS^H, \beta, \varepsilon), \qquad (3)$$

where ω indexes each of the 2^M separate regimes and $V_\omega(\cdot)$ represents the corresponding conditional indirect utility function. Unless preferences are quasilinear or homothetic in income, no closed form solution exists for CS^H, and iterative techniques such as numerical bisection are required to solve for CS^H. However, as discussed by PKH, procedures such as numerical bisection require that the analyst solve the consumer's problem at each iteration conditional on an arbitrary set of (p, Q, y, ε) values. PKH propose a strategy for accomplishing this task that calculates each of the possible 2^M conditional indirect utility functions and ascertains which is the maximum. Although this strategy is computationally feasible for small M, it quickly becomes intractable as M grows large. For example, in our subsequent empirical application where M equals 62, the number of possible regimes is 4.6×10^{18}.

An additional complication with constructing welfare estimates is that the analyst does not observe ε. This limitation suggests that the analyst cannot determine the individual's Hicksian consumer surplus precisely and can at best construct an estimate of the welfare measure's central tendency over the support of ε such as its expectation, $E(CS^H)$. As described in PKH, constructing $E(CS^H)$ requires the use of Monte Carlo techniques that involve simulating several realizations of ε from its estimated distribution, solving for the CS^H conditional on each simulated ε, and averaging the simulated values of CS^H. Increasing the number of simulations improves the precision of the estimate but also increases the computational time involved.

One final notable difficulty arises because these welfare estimates are functions of estimates of β and Σ that are random variables from the analyst's perspective. Quantifying the implications of uncertainty about the parameters' true values by constructing standard errors for the welfare estimates requires replication of the entire simulation routine for several alternative parameter estimates.

The above discussion suggests the significant computation challenges arising with welfare estimation from demand system applications with large choice sets. For welfare measurement to be viable from demand system models, the analyst must be able to quickly solve for the utility the individual obtains conditional on (p, Q, y, ε). As discussed in the introduction, the difficulties associated with this task as well as the difficulties associated with estimating demand system models have led researchers in the outdoor recreation literature to abandon demand system models and instead rely on the discrete choice framework.[2] In the next section, we develop econometrically tractable preference specifications that can be used to model the demand for a large set of quality differentiated goods and to construct Hicksian welfare measures.

3. Preference Specifications and Estimation Strategies

In this paper our approach to modeling consumer choice within the Kuhn-Tucker demand system framework relies on the assumption that consumer preferences are additively separable in each element of x and z. Although PKH employ this assumption in their empirical work, we note that it is a strong preference restriction; it rules out *a priori* inferior goods and implies that all goods are Hicksian substitutes (see Pollak and Wales [1992] for a discussion). We suggest, however, that this assumption implies restrictions on consumer behavior that parallel the implications of discrete choice RUM models. Whereas our demand system specifications assume additive separability, the discrete choice models assume that the consumer's time horizon of choice can be decomposed into separable choice occasions. Additive separability in a systems framework implies that all goods are Hicksian substitutes with non-negative Engel curves, while the discrete choice framework assumes that on a given choice occasion all goods are quality-adjusted perfect substitutes and, with rare exception, income effects are absent.[3]

Specifically, our empirical demand system specifications can be nested within the following general structure:

$$U(\boldsymbol{x},\boldsymbol{Q},z,\boldsymbol{\beta},\boldsymbol{\varepsilon}) = \sum_{j}^{M} \Psi(\boldsymbol{s},\boldsymbol{d}_j,\boldsymbol{\varepsilon})(\phi(\boldsymbol{q}_j)x_j + \theta)^{\rho_j} + z^{\rho_z}$$

$$\ln \Psi(\boldsymbol{s},\boldsymbol{d}_j,\boldsymbol{\varepsilon}) = (\delta + \varepsilon_\delta)^{\mathrm{T}}\boldsymbol{s} + (\zeta + \varepsilon_\zeta)^{\mathrm{T}}\boldsymbol{d}_j + \varepsilon_j \qquad (4)$$

$$\ln \phi(\boldsymbol{q}_j) = \gamma^{\mathrm{T}}\boldsymbol{q}_j$$

where $\boldsymbol{s}$ and $\boldsymbol{d}_j$ are vectors of individual specific demographic variables and site specific dummy variables, respectively, $(\theta, \rho_j, \rho_z, \delta, \zeta, \gamma)$ are estimable parameters, $(\varepsilon_\delta, \varepsilon_\zeta)$ represent unobserved heterogeneity that varies randomly across individuals in the population, and ε_j is unobserved heterogeneity that varies randomly across individuals and goods.

Our preference structure is a close relative of the additively separable linear expenditure system employed by PKH but differs in three important respects. First, our specification can be interpreted as a more general specification because in the limit as all ρ parameters approach zero, our specification nests the linear expenditure system. Second, PKH assume that a good's quality attributes enter through its Ψ parameter. This approach to introducing quality implies that weak complementarity (i.e., $\partial U / \partial \boldsymbol{q}_j = 0$ if $x_j = 0$) is not in general satisfied unless $\theta = 1$ (see Mäler

10

[1974] and Bradford and Hildebrand [1977] for discussions). Because our specification introduces quality through simple repackaging parameters $\phi(\cdot)$ (e.g., Griliches [1964]), weak complementarity is satisfied for all parameter values. Finally, our specification allows the parameters for the demographic and dummy variables entering the Ψ parameters to vary randomly across individuals in the population. As discussed below, this feature of our model allows us to introduce a more flexible structure for unobserved heterogeneity.

Maximizing the utility function in equation (4) with respect to $\boldsymbol{p}^{\mathsf{T}}\boldsymbol{x} + z = y$ and the non-negativity constraints implies a set of first order conditions that, with some manipulation, can be written:

$$\varepsilon_j \leq -(\delta + \varepsilon_\delta)^{\mathsf{T}}\boldsymbol{s} - (\zeta + \varepsilon_\zeta)^{\mathsf{T}}\boldsymbol{d}_j + \ln\frac{\rho_z}{\rho_j} + \ln\frac{p_j}{\phi(q_j)} + (\rho_z - 1)\ln(y - \sum_j p_j x_j) +$$
$$(1 - \rho_j)\ln(\phi(q_j)x_j + \theta) \; \forall j. \tag{5}$$

These weak inequalities, along with assumptions for the distributions of $(\varepsilon_\delta, \varepsilon_\zeta, \varepsilon_j)$, permit estimation of the structural parameters using maximum likelihood techniques. In our application we assume that each ε_j is an independent and identically distributed draw from the type I extreme value distribution with common scale parameter μ. Defining the right hand side of (5) as $g_j(\varepsilon_\delta, \varepsilon_\zeta)$, the likelihood of observing a particular vector of choices $\boldsymbol{x}$ conditional on $(\varepsilon_\delta, \varepsilon_\zeta)$ can be written:

$$l(\boldsymbol{x} \mid \varepsilon_\delta, \varepsilon_\zeta) = \mid \boldsymbol{J} \mid \prod_j \left[[1_{x_j > 0} \times \exp(-g_j(\varepsilon_\delta, \varepsilon_\zeta)/\mu)/\mu] \times \exp(-\exp(-g_j(\varepsilon_\delta, \varepsilon_\zeta)/\mu)) \right], \tag{6}$$

where $\boldsymbol{J}$ is the Jacobian of transformation. The unconditional likelihood of observing $\boldsymbol{x}$ is

$$l(\boldsymbol{x}) = \int l(\boldsymbol{x} \mid \varepsilon_\delta, \varepsilon_\zeta) f(\varepsilon_\delta, \varepsilon_\zeta) d\varepsilon_\delta d\varepsilon_\zeta, \tag{7}$$

where the integral is over the full support of $(\varepsilon_\delta, \varepsilon_\zeta)$. For our application, we assume that $(\varepsilon_\delta, \varepsilon_\zeta)$ are mean zero random draws from the normal distribution with unequal vectors of scale parameters $(\sigma_\delta, \sigma_\zeta)$ and no correlations. Given these assumptions and the structure of our conditional likelihood function, (7) has no closed form solution and cannot be evaluated using numerical integration techniques unless the dimension of $(\varepsilon_\delta, \varepsilon_\zeta)$ is small. In this paper, we follow common empirical practice in the discrete choice literature (e.g., Revelt and Train [1998]) and use simulation to evaluate (7). Our estimation strategy therefore falls under the rubric of simulated maximum likelihood estimation (e.g., Gourieroux and Monfort [1996]). Although estimation of our random parameters model is more computationally difficult than the fixed parameter model with generalized extreme value unobserved heterogeneity employed by PKH, it is more flexible econometrically. In addition to allowing for heteroskedasticity and correlations in the unobserved heterogeneity across groups of sites as PKH's specification does, our specification also allows for heteroskedasticity across individuals.

4. Welfare Calculation

4.1 Solving the Consumer's Problem

An essential component of constructing Hicksian welfare measures involves evaluating the utility an individual achieves conditional on (p, Q, y, ε). When the dimension of the choice set is large, PKH's strategy of analytically constructing all 2^M possible conditional indirect utility functions and determining which is the maximum is not feasible. In this paper, we pursue an alternative, computationally tractable strategy that numerically solves the Kuhn-Tucker conditions for the optimal consumption levels. These optimal values are then inserted into the direct utility function to ascertain the individual's utility conditional on (p, Q, y, ε).

12

Given our additive separability assumption, solving the consumer's problem is greatly simplified. In particular, the Kuhn-Tucker conditions take the general form:

$$U_j(x_j) \leq U_z(z)p_j, \forall j \tag{8}$$

$$x_j \geq 0, \forall j \tag{9}$$

$$z = y - \sum_j p_j x_j. \tag{10}$$

Note that additive separability implies that only x_j and z enter the jth inequality in (8). This structure suggests that if the analyst knew the optimal value for z, she could use (8) and (9) to solve for each x_j. Therefore, solving for the optimal value of z is equivalent to solving the consumer's problem. Building on this insight, we developed the following numerical bisection algorithm to solve the consumer's problem:

1) At iteration i, set $z_a^i = (z_l^{i-1} + z_h^{i-1})/2$. To initialize the algorithm, set $z_l^0 = 0$ and $z_h^0 = y$.
2) Conditional on z_a^i, solve for x^i using (8) and (9).
3) Use (10) and x^i to construct $\tilde{z}^i$.
4) If $\tilde{z}^i > z_a^i$, set $z_l^i = z_a^i$ & $z_h^i = z_h^{i-1}$. Otherwise, set $z_l^i = z_l^{i-1}$ & $z_h^i = z_a^i$.
5) Iterate until $abs(z_l^i - z_h^i) \leq c$ where c is arbitrarily small. [4]

The ability of this algorithm to solve the consumer's problem relies on the strict concavity of preferences in every argument.[5] By totally differentiating (8), one can show that strict concavity implies that $\partial x_j / \partial z \geq 0$. This inequality, in conjunction with the fact that our model has a unique solution, (x^*, z^*), suggests that $\tilde{z}^i \geq z_a^i$ if $z_a^i \leq z^*$ and conversely, $\tilde{z}^i \leq z_a^i$ if $z_a^i \geq z^*$. Updating the upper and lower bounds using the criteria stipulated in step 4 and iterating solves for (x^*, z^*).[6] Plugging these optimal solutions into (4) allows the analyst to evaluate the consumer's utility conditional on (p, Q, y, ε). Nesting this algorithm for solving the consumer's problem within a numerical bisection routine that iteratively solves for the income compensation that equates utility before and after a price and quality change will allow the analyst to construct

the Hicksian consumer surplus, CS^H.

4.2 Incorporating Observed Choice

The algorithm described in the previous section permits construction of welfare measures

conditional on a set of unobserved heterogeneity values. As discussed in Section 2, a precise

estimate of the individual's Hicksian consumer surplus is not possible because $(\varepsilon_\delta, \varepsilon_\zeta, \boldsymbol{\varepsilon})$ are not

observed. However, using simulation techniques and the distribution of the unobserved

heterogeneity, the analyst can construct estimates of CS^H such as its expectation, $E(CS^H)$.

The approach taken by PKH to simulating the unobserved heterogeneity employs the full

distributional support of $(\varepsilon_\delta, \varepsilon_\zeta, \boldsymbol{\varepsilon})$. In this paper, we build on an approach suggested by von

Haefen [forthcoming] and instead simulate the unobserved heterogeneity from the region of the

unobserved heterogeneity's support that is consistent with the individual's observed choice. In

other words, we simulate $(\varepsilon_\delta, \varepsilon_\zeta, \boldsymbol{\varepsilon})$ such that at baseline conditions our model perfectly predicts

the observed choices we find in our data, and we use the model's structure of substitution to

predict how individuals respond to price, quality, and income changes. This approach contrasts

with PKH's more traditional approach that uses the structure of the model to predict both what

individuals do at baseline conditions as well as how they respond to price, quality, and income

changes. For the purposes of our application in this paper, incorporating observed choice is

appealing because, although it requires the use of more complicated simulation techniques, it

greatly reduces the number of simulations required to produce a precise estimate of $E(CS^H)$ as

well as the computational time involved.[7]

We follow von Haefen and use a sequential strategy to simulate the unobserved

heterogeneity consistent with the individual's observed choice. Note that our objective is to simulate from the distribution of $(\varepsilon_\delta, \varepsilon_\zeta, \boldsymbol{\varepsilon})$ conditional on $\boldsymbol{x}$, $f(\varepsilon_\delta, \varepsilon_\zeta, \boldsymbol{\varepsilon} \mid \boldsymbol{x})$. This distribution can be decomposed as follows:

$$f(\varepsilon_\delta, \varepsilon_\zeta, \boldsymbol{\varepsilon} \mid \boldsymbol{x}) = f(\varepsilon_\delta, \varepsilon_\zeta \mid \boldsymbol{x}) \times f(\boldsymbol{\varepsilon} \mid \varepsilon_\delta, \varepsilon_\zeta, \boldsymbol{x}). \tag{11}$$

Equation (11) states that the joint conditional distribution for the unobserved heterogeneity can be decomposed into the marginal distribution for the random parameters conditional on $\boldsymbol{x}$ multiplied by the conditional distribution for the site specific unobserved heterogeneity conditional on $\boldsymbol{x}$. We use an adaptive Metropolis-Hastings algorithm (Chib and Greenberg [1995]) tailored to our problem to simulate from $f(\varepsilon_\delta, \varepsilon_\zeta \mid \boldsymbol{x})$. The steps of the algorithm are as follows:

1) At iteration i, simulate a candidate vector of unobserved heterogeneity, $(\tilde{\varepsilon}_\delta^i, \tilde{\varepsilon}_\zeta^i)$, from the normal distribution with location parameters $(\varepsilon_\delta^{i-1}, \varepsilon_\zeta^{i-1})$ and scale parameters $(\mathrm{r}^i \sigma_\delta, \mathrm{r}^i \sigma_\zeta)$ where r^i is a constant. To initialize the process, set each element of $(\varepsilon_\delta^0, \varepsilon_\zeta^0)$ equal to zero and r^0 equal to 0.1.

2) Construct the following statistic:
$$\chi^i = \frac{N(\tilde{\varepsilon}_\delta^i / \sigma_\delta, \tilde{\varepsilon}_\zeta^i / \sigma_\zeta) \times l(\boldsymbol{x} \mid \tilde{\varepsilon}_\delta^i, \tilde{\varepsilon}_\zeta^i)}{N(\varepsilon_\delta^{i-1} / \sigma_\delta, \varepsilon_\zeta^{i-1} / \sigma_\zeta) \times l(\boldsymbol{x} \mid \varepsilon_\delta^{i-1}, \varepsilon_\zeta^{i-1})}$$
where $N(\cdot)$ is the probability density function for the normal distribution and $l(\cdot)$ is defined in equation (6). If $\chi^i \geq U$ where U is a uniform random draw, accept the candidate random parameters, i.e., $(\varepsilon_\delta^i, \varepsilon_\zeta^i) = (\tilde{\varepsilon}_\delta^i, \tilde{\varepsilon}_\zeta^i)$. Otherwise, set $(\varepsilon_\delta^i, \varepsilon_\zeta^i) = (\varepsilon_\delta^{i-1}, \varepsilon_\zeta^{i-1})$.

3) Gelman et al. [1995] argue that the Metropolis-Hastings algorithm for the normal distribution is most efficient if the acceptance rate of candidate parameters is between 0.23 and 0.44. Accordingly, we employ the following updating rule for r^i. If the proportion of accepted candidate parameters is less than 0.3, set $r^{i+1} = (1.1) \times r^i$. Otherwise, set $r^{i+1} = (0.9) \times r^i$.

4) Iterate.

After a burn-in period, this Monte Carlo, Markov Chain simulator generates random draws from $f(\varepsilon_\delta, \varepsilon_\zeta \mid \boldsymbol{x})$.

After values of $(\varepsilon_\delta, \varepsilon_\zeta)$ are simulated, drawing from $f(\varepsilon \mid \varepsilon_\delta, \varepsilon_\zeta, \boldsymbol{x})$ is far simpler. If good j is consumed in a strictly positive quantity, the structure of our model, the simulated random parameters, and the individual's observed choice imply that $\varepsilon_j^i = g_j(\varepsilon_\delta^i, \varepsilon_\zeta^i)$, where $g_j(\cdot)$ is the right hand side of equation (5). Otherwise, ε_j^i can be simulated from the truncated type I extreme value distribution via

$$\varepsilon_j^i = -\ln(-\ln(\exp(-\exp(-g_j(\varepsilon_\delta^i, \varepsilon_\zeta^i) / \mu)) \times U))) \times \mu,$$

where U again is a uniform random draw.

4.3 Summary

Before proceeding to the data and empirical results, we summarize the key components of our welfare measurement algorithm:

1) For simulation i, use the sequential procedure described in the previous section to simulate $(\varepsilon_\delta, \varepsilon_\zeta, \varepsilon_j)$ consistent with the individual's observed choice. Because simulating from $f(\varepsilon_\delta, \varepsilon_\zeta \mid \boldsymbol{x})$ requires the use of an adaptive Metropolis-Hastings algorithm, discard the first T simulations.
2) For simulation $i > T$, use a numerical bisection routine to solve for the simulated Hicksian consumer surplus associated with a price and quality change.
2a) At each step of the numerical bisection routine that solves for the Hicksian consumer surplus associated with simulation i, use the numerical bisection routine described in Section 4.1 to solve the consumer's problem. Inserting these optimal values into (4) permits the analyst to determine the utility the individual achieves.
3) Average each of the simulated Hicksian consumer surplus values to construct an estimate of $E(CS^H)$, the individual's expected Hicksian consumer surplus.

Although our algorithm for estimating welfare measures has multiple layers and numerous details, our experience has been that it is surprisingly easy and fast to use in an applied setting. One of the algorithm's most appealing attributes is that each of its steps can be executed simultaneously for every observation in the sample using vector and matrix notation. This feature implies that coding and executing the algorithm in a matrix programming language reduces the computational burden significantly.

16

5. Application

We apply our demand systems framework to a random sample of Delaware residents' recreational day trips to Mid-Atlantic ocean beaches in 1997. From a policy perspective, understanding beach recreation demand is important for at least two reasons. Oil and toxic spills in coastal waters often result in beach closings. Under the Oil Pollution Act of 1990 and other Natural Resource Damage Assessment (NRDA) statutes, the public's lost economic benefits arising from these spills are compensable. Deacon and Kolstad [2000] discuss issues associated with estimating these losses and argue that revealed preference recreation demand models are a preferred method for ascertaining beach users' resource values. Furthermore, understanding how the characteristics of beaches such as beach width influence the demand for beach recreation can help inform the ongoing debate over beach nourishment as a strategy for combating coastal erosion. Beach nourishment is a technically feasible but costly way to maintain coastal areas threatened by erosion from rising sea levels, development, and natural causes. At present, substantial state and federal resources have been earmarked for these activities in response to a perceived need to protect tourism and recreation related infrastructure.[8]

To assess the recreational values of beach amenities and to gauge residents' willingness to pay for beach quality improvements such as nourishment, researchers at the University of Delaware collected data on visits by Delaware residents to 62 ocean beaches in New Jersey, Delaware, Maryland, and Virginia during 1997. Figure 1 shows a map of the region and several of the major beaches included in the data set. Massey [2001] discusses the data collection effort in detail. A mail survey of 1000 randomly selected Delaware residents resulted in 540 completed responses. Although respondents provided information on the number of day trips, overnight trips, and side trips made to each of the 62 beaches, we follow conventional empirical practice in the recreation literature and consider only day trips in our analysis.

The survey collected sufficient information to compute round trip travel costs to each of the beaches. For every individual in the sample, a beach's price is assumed to consist of transit costs (valued at $0.35 per mile), beach fees, highway tolls, parking fees, a ferry toll on trips from southern Delaware to New Jersey beaches, and the opportunity cost of travel time valued at the individual's average wage rate. Distances and travel times to each of the sixty-two sites from each of 540 residents' homes were calculated using *PC Miler*. The wage rate was estimated as the individual's annual income divided by 2040 (i.e., the typical number of hours worked in a year).

Household characteristic and demographic data were also collected and are used to parameterize our utility function. Household specific variables and recreational summary statistics are listed and described in the top part of table 1. Note that respondents took on average 9.77 trips and visited 2.77 different beaches during the season. The maximum number of beaches visited by a respondent was nineteen, and 165 people surveyed (30% of the sample) did not visit a beach during the season.

In addition to the behavioral data, auxiliary information on the characteristics of the sixty-two beaches was also gathered. Fourteen variables are used to differentiate the beaches included in the study. These variables are listed and described in the lower part of table 1. Of most interest for policy purposes are the indicator variables for wide and narrow beach. Of the 62 beaches, 25% are wide (i.e., greater than 200 feet in width) and 14% are narrow (less than 75 feet in width). The impacts of the wide and narrow dummy variables on the demand for beach visits will allow us to gauge the effects of beach width on recreation demand and to assess the welfare implications of policies designed to alter beach width such as beach nourishment.

6. *Parameter Estimates*

Although we estimated several demand system specifications consistent with the generic structure described in Section 3, we present a representative set of our findings in this section. Table 1 contains estimates for two fixed parameter models (i.e. $\varepsilon_\delta = \varepsilon_\varsigma = 0$) nested in equation (4): a translated CES specification (column 2) resulting from the restrictions $\rho_z = \rho_j = \rho \,\forall j$ and a second specification (column 3) resulting from the restriction $\rho_j = 0 \,\forall j$. Table 2 contains estimates for more general random parameter versions of these specifications that allow the parameters in the Ψ index to vary randomly across the population. Although the parameter estimates in Table 1 are estimated with conventional maximum likelihood techniques, the parameter estimates in table 2 are obtained via simulated maximum likelihood procedures. To improve simulation efficiency we follow common empirical practice in the discrete choice literature and employ 250 Halton draws rather than random draws in the calculation of our simulated probabilities. Train [1999] demonstrates that for many random parameters models Halton draws outperform random draws in terms of the number of simulations needed to achieve an arbitrary level of precision.

In general we find statistically significant, plausibly signed and robust coefficient estimates for the four models. For example we find that age negatively impacts trips to all destinations while ownership of vacation property in Delaware is positively related to increased beach visitation. Respondents with children of all ages tend to take more trips than respondent with no kids, although this result is not significant for all models. Students and retired indivduals also tend to take more trips. Several site characteristics are also statistically significant determinants of choice. Of most interest for policy purposes are the signs on the narrow and wide beach dummy variables. We find for all four models negative and statistically significant coefficient estimates for both of these variables, suggesting that respondents prefer beaches of moderate width. This finding is consistent with Parsons et al.'s [1999] empirical findings and suggests that individuals dislike narrow beaches with limited available recreation area and wide beaches that require long walks to the waterfront.

For both specifications the fixed parameter results are nested versions of the random parameter results, allowing direct comparisons of the likelihood function values to determine the contribution of the random parameters to the model fit. In both cases we find substantial increases in likelihood values with the addition of random parameters, suggesting the importance in this application of allowing for additional unobserved heterogeneity in the characterization of preferences. This finding is further supported by noting that seven of eight and six of eight of the parameters' standard error estimates are statistically significant in each of the specifications, respectively. A direct comparison of the log-likelihood values for the translated CES and the second specification is not appropriate since the models are not nested. However, since the models are both restricted versions of the same more general specification a likelihood dominance criteria (Pollak and Wales [1991]) can be used to gauge their comparative fits. We find for both the fixed and random parameter specifications that the second specification fits the data best, suggesting on statistical grounds that our second random parameters specifications provides the best characterization of preferences in this application.

7. *Welfare Analysis*

The parameter estimates allow welfare analysis for our beach application employing the methods described in section 4. We analyze three scenarios designed to provide different types of valuation information for beach recreation and to provide a demonstration of the feasibility of our welfare analysis computations. Two pertain to the recreation value lost when beaches close, and the third addresses the recreational loses associated with beach erosion. The specific scenarios analyzed include:

- Closing of Rehoboth Beach
- Closing of northern Delaware beaches
- Lost beach width at all Maryland, Delaware, and Virginia (MD/DE/VA) developed beaches.

These three scenarios have policy relevance for the mid-Atlantic region. Oil tankers enter the Delaware Bay regularly and pass near the most frequently visited ocean beaches in the state. The possibility of a spill and consequent closure of beaches, especially along the northernmost beaches from Cape Henlopen State Park to the Delaware Seashore State Park (see Figure 1), is widely recognized. For example the June 1989 Presidente Rivera oil spill off the New Jersey coast would have resulted in beach closures had it occurred further south near the mouth of the Delaware Bay. In our analysis the first two scenarios simulate the welfare loss that might be associated with such a spill. We consider the closure of Rehoboth Beach, located along the northern Delaware coast, because it is the most visited beach in the state. We also consider the closure of all beaches from Cape Henlopen State Park to the Delaware Seashore State Park. These are seven of the 62 beaches in our analysis and comprise the eleven northernmost miles of Delaware's twenty-five miles of ocean beaches. In our judgement this is the set of beaches most likely to experience the effects of a spill.

Our third scenario pertains to beach erosion on the MD/DE/VA beaches, a major policy issue in the region. For more than twenty years the three states have pumped sand onto their beaches to maintain beach width in support of recreation uses. The projects are costly and controversial and recreation benefit analyses associated with them are rather limited and outdated. Using our estimated model, we simulate the welfare loss associated with all developed beaches in the MD/DE/VA area eroding to a width of seventy-five feet. This will affect most of the popular beaches in the area. While a more severe erosion scenario is possible, this one seems both plausible and within the range of our data. These losses, of course, approximate the recreation gains associated with a nourishment project assuming that full beach migration is not a policy option. In our scenario all the natural (park) beaches are assumed to maintain their current width. These beaches tend to migrate inland naturally and maintain width.

Point estimates and standard errors for the three welfare scenarios (1997 dollars per respondent per season) are presented in table 4. Columns 2 and 3 present the translated CES and second specification estimates, respectively. To evaluate whether our demand system models generate qualitatively different policy inference from the discrete choice RUM-based strategies that dominate current empirical practice, column 4 presents welfare estimates from repeated discrete choice RUM models (e.g., Morey, Rowe, and Watson [1993]) that are generated by the conditional welfare measurement procedure outlined in von Haefen [forthcoming].[9] These models assume: 1) the recreation season can be decomposed into 75 separable and statistically independent choice occasions;[10] 2) each individual on each choice occasion makes a discrete choice among the 62 sites and an option not to recreate, 3) preferences for a site (the outside alternative) are a linear additive index of its price, attributes, (demographic variables) and an i.i.d. type I extreme value random draw; and 4) a subset of the parameters entering the indexes are independently normally distributed across the population. A table with parameter estimates for the specifications we consider in this paper is available from the authors upon request.

For each scenario fixed and random parameter model estimates are presented together for comparison purposes. In all cases the estimates have plausible magnitudes and standard errors that suggest statistically significant differences from zero. Additionally, a few general patterns emerge. Perhaps the most striking is that the inclusion of random coefficients decreases the magnitude of the estimated welfare effects for all models and all scenarios. This is consistent with some empirical findings in other applications of the random parameters framework (e.g. Petrin [2001], Phaneuf et al. [1998]) and suggests that the additional unobserved heterogeneity introduced by random parameter models allows for a greater degree of substitution among goods and, as a result, smaller (absolute) economic values. Next, in spite of the statistical dominance of the second specification over the translated CES specification, both demand system specifications provide qualitatively similar welfare measures for both the fixed and random parameters versions. Finally, there are some differences between estimates for the demand system models and the repeated discrete choice models, although not for all scenarios. For the random parameters specifications, welfare estimates for the closing of Rehoboth Beach differ substantially across the modeling frameworks but are less dramatic for the other scenarios.

8. Conclusion

Our general conclusion from the research presented in this paper is that the demand system framework represents a viable strategy for modeling consumer choice and generating Hicksian welfare measures for individual or household level applications with many quality-differentiated goods. Using Monte Carlo estimation and welfare construction procedures, we present empirical results from a beach recreation application that demonstrate how this can be accomplished. Our methodological approach and empirical findings suggest that the demand system framework represents a genuine alternative to the RUM-based strategies that dominate current empirical practice. Moreover, the demand system approach has the conceptual advantage of combining the intensive and extensive margins of consumer choice in a behaviorally consistent framework.

Numerous extensions to our approach are possible, and we discuss two in closing. Relaxing the assumption that preferences are additively separable that is central to our modeling strategy represents a significant area for future work. From a computational perspective, relaxing additive separability without jeopardizing the demand system framework's tractability in estimation and welfare construction for applications with many goods represents a formidable task. However, with continued advances in the computational performance of personal computers, progress in this area is possible. In addition, our structure of the consumer's problem assumes that there are combinations of prices, site attributes, and income that would make every individual participate in some form of beach recreation and visit each of the different sites. Introspection suggests, however, that some individuals may not participate in beach recreation or visit a particular site under any circumstances. Therefore, a significant modeling innovation would be to augment our framework with a model of the individual's decision to participate in any form of beach recreation as well as her decision to consider visiting each of the quality differentiated sites.

References

Bockstael, Nancy E., W. Michael Hanemann, and Catherine L. Kling. "Estimating the Value of Water Quality Improvements in a Recreational Demand Framework." *Water Resources Research*, 23(1987): 951-960.

Bockstael, N., I. Strand, and K. McConnell. "Benefits from Improvements in Chesapeake Bay Water Quality". *Volume II of Benefit Analysis Using Indirect or Imputed Market Methods.* EPA Contract No. CR-811043-01-0, 1988.

Berry, S., Levinsohn, J., and A. Pakes. "Automobile Prices in Market Equilibrium," *Econometrica*, 63(1995): 841-890.

Bradford, D., and G. Hildebrandt. "Observable Preferences for Public Goods," *Journal of Public Economics* 8(1977): 111-131.

Chib, S. and E. Greenberg, "Understanding the Metropolis-Hastings Algorithm," *American Statistician* 49(1995): 327-335.

Deacon, R. and C. Kolstad, "Valuing Beach Recreation Lost in Environmental Accidents," *Journal of Water Resources Planning and Management* 126(2000): 374-381.

Edwards, Steven F. and Frank J. Gable. "Estimating the Value of Beach Recreation from Property Values: An Exploration with Comparisons to Nourishment Costs." *Ocean & Shoreline Management*, 15 (1991): 37-55.

Environmental Economics Research Group. "Natural Resource Damage Assessment for the Tampa Bay Oil Spill: Recreational Use Losses for Florida Residents." Report prepared for the Florida Department of Environmental Protection, 1998.

Feather, P., D. Hellerstein, and T. Tomasi. "A Discrete-Count Model of Recreation Demand," *Journal of Environmental Economics and Management*, 29(1995): 214-227.

Gelman, A. et al. *Bayesian Data Analysis.* Chapman & Hall: London, UK, 1995.

Griliches, Zvi. "Notes on the Measurement of Price and Quality Changes," in *Models of Income Determination, NBER Studies in Income and Wealth, Volume 28*, Princeton, NJ: Princeton University Press, 1964.

Gourieroux, C. and A. Monfort. *Simulation-Based Econometric Methods*. New York: Oxford University Press, 1996.

Hausman, J. A., G. K. Leonard, and D. McFadden. "A Utility-Consistent, Combined Discrete Choice and Count Data Model: Assessing Recreational Use Losses Due to Natural Resource Damage." *Journal of Public Economics*, 56(1995): 1-30.

Hendel, I, "Estimating Multiple-Discrete Choice Models: An Application to Computerization," *Review of Economic Studies* 66(1999): 423-446.

Herriges, J. and C. Kling. "Nonlinear Income Effects in Random Utility Models," *Review of Economics and Statistics* 81(1999): 62-72.

Lee, L.F. and M. Pitt, "Microeconomic Demand Systems with Binding Non-Negativity Constraints: The Dual Approach," *Econometrica* 54(1986): 1237-42.

Leeworthy, Vernon R. and Peter C. Wiley. "Recreational Use Value for Three Southern California Beaches." Strategic Environmental Assessments Division, Office of Ocean Resource Conservation and Assessment, National Oceanic and Atmospheric Administration, Rockville, Maryland, 1993.

Mäler, Karl-Göran. *Environmental Economics: A Theoretical Inquiry*. Baltimore, MD: Johns Hopkins University Press for Resources for the Future, 1974.

Massey, D. Matthew. "Heterogeneous Preferences in Random Utility Models of Recreation Demand." Ph.D. Dissertation, University of Delaware, 2001.

McConnell, Kenneth E. "Congestion and Willingness to Pay: A Study of Beach Use." *Land Economics*, 53(1977): 185-195.

McConnell, K. E. "Household Labor Market Choices and the Demand for Recreation." *Land Economics*, 75(1999): 466-477

McFadden, D. "Conditional Logit Analysis of Qualitative Choice Behavior," in *Frontiers in Econometrics*, Paul Zarembka, Editor. Academic Press: New York, 1974.

McFadden, D. "Economic Choices," *American Economic Review*, 91(2001): 351-378.

Morey, E., R. Rowe, and M. Watson, "A Repeated Nested-Logit Model of Atlantic Salmon Fishing," *American Journal of Agricultural Economics* 75(1993): 578-592.

Neary, J. and K. Roberts. "The Theory of Household Behavior under Rationing," *European Economic Review* 13(1980): 25-42.

Nevo, A. "Mergers with Differentiated Products: The Case of the Ready-to-Eat Cereal Industry," *Rand Journal of Economics* 31(2000): 395-421.

Parsons, G., P. Jakus, and T. Tomasi: "A Comparison of Welfare Estimates from Four Models for Linking Seasonal Recreation Trips to Multinomial Logit Models of Choice," *Journal of Environmental Economics and Management*, 38(1999): 143-157.

Parsons, G., and M.J. Kealy: "A Demand Theory for Number of Trips in a Random Utility Model of Recreation," *Journal of Environmental Economics and Management*, 29(1995): 357-367.

Parsons, G., D.M. Massey, and T. Tomasi. "Familiar and Favorite Sites in a Random Utility Model of Beach Recreation," *Marine Resource Economics* 14(1999): 299-315.

Petrin, A. "Quantifying the Benefits of New Products: the Case of the Mini-Vans," working paper, University of Chicago, 2001.

Phaneuf, D.J., C.L. Kling, and J.A. Herriges. "Estimation and Welfare Calculations in a Generalized Corner Solution Model with an Application to Recreation Demand," *Review of Economics and Statistics* 82(2000): 83-92.

Phaneuf, D., C. Kling, and J. Herriges, "Valuing Water Quality Improvements Using Revealed Preference Methods When Corner Solutions are Present," *American Journal of Agricultural Economics* 80(200): 1025-1031.

Phaneuf, D.J., "A Dual Approach to Modeling Corner Solutions in Recreation Demand," *Journal of Environmental Economics and Management* 37(1999): 85-105.

Pollak, R. and T. Wales, "The Likelihood Dominance Criteria," *Journal of Econometrics* 47(1991): 227-242.

Pollak, R. and T. Wales. *Demand System Specification and Estimation*. New York: Oxford University Press, 1992.

Revelt, D. and K. Train, "Mixed Logit with Repeated Choices: Households' Choices of Appliance Efficiency Level," *Review of Economics and Statistics* 80(1998): 658-663.

Silberman, Jonathan, Daniel A. Gerlowski, and Nancy A. Williams. "Estimating Existence Value for Users and Nonusers of New Jersey Beaches." *Land Economics*, 68(1992): 225-236.

Small, K. and H. Rosen, "Applied Welfare Economics with Discrete Choice Models," *Econometrica* 49(1981): 105-130.

Smith, V.K. and R. Palmquist, "Temporal Substitution and the Recreational Value of Coastal Amenities," *Review of Economics and Statistics* 76(1994): 119-126.

Smith, V. Kerry, Xiaolong Zhang, and Raymond B. Palmquists. "Marine Debris, Beach Quality, and Non-Market Values." *Environmental and Resource Economics*, 10(1997): 223-247.

Train, K. "Halton Sequences for Mixed Logit," working paper, 1999.

von Haefen, R. "Incorporating Observed Choice into the Construction of Welfare Measures from Random Utility Models," *Journal of Environmental Economics and Management*, Forthcoming.

Wales, T. and A. Woodland, "Estimation of Consumer Demand Systems with Binding Non-Negativity Constraints," *Journal of Econometrics* 21(1983): 263-285.

Wilman, E. A., "Hedonic Prices and Beach Recreational Values," in *Advances in Applied Microeconomics*, V. Kerry Smith, Editor. JAI Press, Inc.: Greenwich, CT, 1981.

Notes

[1] For a review and empirical comparison of these models, see Parsons, Jakus, and Tomasi [1999].

[2] Researchers in other fields of economics have also abandoned the demand system framework when modeling consumer choice for many goods. For examples of this trend in the new empirical IO literature see Berry, Levinsohn and Pakes [1995], Hendel [1999], and Nevo [2001].

[3] For a notable application with income effects, see Herriges and Kling [1999].

[4] We note that the basic numerical bisection algorithm described here can be partially modified in numerous ways and still produce the optimal solutions. Our experience suggested that our algorithm was the fastest relative to numerous variations of it.

[5] The assumptions of strict quasi-concavity and additive separability imply strict concavity (e.g., Pollak and Wales [1992]).

[6] We have also compared our algorithm for constructing the individual's utility to the procedure suggested by PKH with a low dimensional choice set and found no difference between the two up to eight digits of numerical precision.

[7] Based on some Monte Carlo experiments with low dimensional choice sets, we found that the unconditional approach to welfare measurement required roughly three times as many simulations to generate precise estimates relative to the conditional approach. In terms of total computational run-time, the conditional welfare estimates took roughly one-third the time to generate.

[8] Several studies have attempted to value beach access or beach use in general. A few have also attempted to value beach characteristics such as beach width. These studies have tended to be contingent valuation or simple single site travel-cost models. Examples of contingent valuation applications include McConnell [1977], Smith, Zhang, and Palmquist [1997] and Silberman, Gerlowski, and Williams [1992]. Examples of single site travel-cost models are Leeworthy and Wiley [1993] and McConnell [1999]. There have also been a few travel-cost random utility maximization (RUM) models. Bockstael, Hanemann, and Kling [1987] and Bockstael, Strand, and McConnell [1988] are examples of early work applying the RUM framework to beach recreation. More recent applications include Parsons, Massey, and Tomasi [1999] and Environmental Economics Research Group [1998]. Finally, there have been a few hedonic price applications treating proximity to beaches as a characteristic of coastal property markets from which beach values have been inferred. Examples of these are Edwards and Gable [1991], Wilman [1981], and Smith and Palmquist [1994].

[9] Although it is somewhat arbitrary to use the repeated discrete choice RUM model to compare our demand system models to the alternative RUM-based models, we note that Parsons, Jakus, and Tomasi [1998] found qualitatively similar welfare estimates across four alternative discrete choice RUM models applied to a common data set.

[10] An arbitrary feature of the repeated discrete choice framework is the number of choice occasions. We specified 75 choice occasions because no one in our sample took more than 75 trips. Our experimentation with alternative specifications of the number of choice occasions suggested that welfare estimates were largely insensitive to this arbitrary judgement.

Table 1: Household and Beach Characteristics Variables

Variable	Description	Summary[a]
Household specific variables		
Ln(age)	Natural log of respondent age	3.82 (0.33)
Kids under 10	Respondent has kids under 10 (0/1)	0.26
Kids 10 to 16	Respondent has kids between 10 and 16 (0/1)	0.20
Vacation property in DE	Respondent owns vacation home in DE (0/1)	0.03
Retired	Respondent is retired (0/1)	0.24
Student	Respondent is student (0/1)	0.05
Income	Household annual income	49,944 (30,295)
Trips	Total visits for day trips to all sites	9.77 (14.06)
Sites visited	Number of beaches visited during 1997	2.70 (3.19)
Site characteristics[b]		
Beach length	Length of beach in miles	0.62 (0.87)
Boardwalk	Boardwalk with shops and attractions (0/1)	0.40
Amusements	Amusement park near beach (0/1)	0.13
Private/limited access	Access limited (0/1)	0.25
Park	State or federal park or wildlife refuge (0/1)	0.09
Wide Beach	Beach is more than 200 feet wide (0/1)	0.25
Narrow Beach	Beach is less than 75 feet wide (0/1)	0.14
Atlantic City	Atlantic city indicator (0/1)	0.016
Surfing	Recognized as good surfing location (0/1)	0.35
High Rise	Highly developed beach front (0/1)	0.24
Park within	Part of the beach is a park area (0/1)	0.14
Facility	Bathrooms available (0/1)	0.48
Parking	Public parking available (0/1)	0.45
New Jersey Beach	New Jersey beach indicator (0/1)	0.74
Price	Person-specific money and time cost of travel	$118[c]

[a]Summary statistics for household variables are means (standard deviations) over the 540 individuals. Summary statistics for site variables are means (standard deviations) over the 62 sites.

[b] We thank Tony Pratt and Michael Powell of the Department of Natural Resources and Environmental Control and Steve Hafner of Coastal Research Center at Richard Stockton College of New Jersey for their help in compiling and verify the characteristic data.

[c]Each individual in the sample of 540 has a unique trip cost to each of the 62 sites. This statistic is the mean of the mean of the individual trip prices. Since prices are based on distance there is substantial variability in individual prices for the set of sites and individual prices across the sample for a given site.

Table 2: Kuhn-Tucker Fixed Parameter Estimates[a]

	#1 Translated CES	#2
Log-Likelihood	-7,837.40	-7,676.21
Ψ_i Index Parameters		
Constant	-3.8169 (-3.480)	2.2443 (1.744)
ln(Age)	-0.5822 (-2.142)	-0.5356 (-2.141)
Kids under 10	0.0593 (0.463)	0.0686 (0.596)
Kids 10 to 16	0.1996 (1.376)	0.1960 (1.465)
Vacation Property in DE	0.7924 (3.696)	0.9318 (4.700)
Retired	0.3611 (1.787)	0.0566 (0.302)
Student	0.4328 (2.140)	0.2906 (1.549)
Park	-0.0589 (-0.744)	-0.0671 (-0.857)
New Jersey Beach	-1.4401 (-8.900)	-1.2213 (-8.785)
Translating Parameter		
θ	3.5132 (9.693)	4.9187 (10.954)
Simple Repackaging Quality Index Parameters		
Beach Length (Miles)	0.0726 (1.843)	0.0764 (2.034)
Boardwalk	-0.2199 (-2.670)	-0.2020 (-2.589)
Amusements	0.8568 (9.178)	0.7551 (8.650)
Private/Limited Access	-0.6099 (-5.739)	-0.5750 (-5.816)
Wide Beach	-0.2286 (-2.999)	-0.1901 (-2.654)
Narrow Beach	-0.4088 (-3.141)	-0.3729 (-3.011)
Atlantic City	0.7657 (7.100)	0.6994 (7.212)
Surfing	0.1805 (2.235)	0.1554 (1.997)
High Rise	0.1206 (1.415)	0.1331 (1.671)
Park Within	0.5775 (6.220)	0.5256 (5.930)
Facility	-0.0347 (-0.582)	-0.0275 (-0.463)
Parking	0.4996 (5.126)	0.4667 (4.819)
Rho Parameters		
$\ln \rho$	-1.6185 (-6.189)	-
$\ln \rho_z$	-	-0.3063 (-3.105)
Type I Extreme Value Scale Parameter		
μ	0.8759 (19.241)	0.8080 (22.867)

[a]t-statistics based on robust standard errors reported in parentheses

Table 3: Kuhn-Tucker Random Parameter Estimates[a]

	#1 Translated CES		#2	
Log-Likelihood	-6,828.73		-6,780.62	
Ψ_i Index Parameters				
	Mean	Std. Dev.	Mean	Std. Dev.
Constant	-3.5091	-	1.2164	-
	(-8.339)		(1.359)	
ln(Age)	-0.4734	0.2361	-0.2535	0.2022
	(-4.235)	(19.663)	(-1.711)	(25.258)
Kids under 10	0.1042	0.0601	0.1431	0.2090
	(1.957)	(1.008)	(2.106)	(2.894)
Kids 10 to 16	0.0245	0.3576	-0.0404	0.1203
	(0.370)	(7.719)	(-0.399)	(1.124)
Vacation Property in DE	0.9008	0.2248	0.8610	0.1626
	(14.556)	(3.065)	(7.363)	(2.505)
Retired	0.1288	0.1806	-0.2505	0.2116
	(1.018)	(4.774)	(-2.520)	(4.808)
Student	0.4337	0.6611	0.4032	0.0923
	(4.676)	(7.604)	(1.259)	(0.907)
Park	-0.0828	0.3266	-0.0823	0.3633
	(-1.321)	(5.607)	(-1.405)	(6.643)
New Jersey Beach	-1.0095	1.0346	-0.9697	0.8661
	(-7.871)	(11.553)	(-9.915)	(17.279)

Translating Parameter

θ	6.0443 (13.484)	7.4472 (15.430)

Simple Repackaging Quality Index Parameters

Beach Length (Miles)	0.0806 (3.431)	0.0810 (3.464)
Boardwalk	-0.0527 (-0.961)	-0.0516 (-0.972)
Amusements	0.6200 (9.275)	0.5989 (9.337)
Private/Limited Access	-0.3893 (-6.685)	-0.3904 (-6.853)
Wide Beach	-0.1677 (-3.279)	-0.1590 (-3.112)
Narrow Beach	-0.2431 (-3.228)	-0.2406 (-3.210)
Atlantic City	0.5373 (6.084)	0.5403 (6.136)
Surfing	0.1040 (1.974)	0.1015 (1.939)
High Rise	-0.0413 (-0.736)	-0.0252 (-0.472)
Park Within	0.3931 (5.874)	0.3859 (5.727)
Facility	-0.0119 (-0.342)	-0.0101 (-0.305)
Parking	0.2664 (4.011)	0.2620 (4.129)

Rho Parameters

$\ln \rho$	-1.9391 (-7.919)	-
$\ln \rho_z$	-	-0.4294 (-4.276)

Type I Extreme Value Scale Parameter

μ	0.4044 (23.189)	0.4011 (26.459)

[a] t-statistics based on robust standard errors in parentheses. Simulated probabilities computed using 250 Halton draws.

Table 4: Mean Seasonal Welfare Estimates (1997 Dollars)[a]

	#1 Translated CES	#2	Repeated Discrete Choice
Closing of Rehoboth Beach			
Fixed Coefficients	-$81.13	-$93.69	-$83.09
	(7.11)	(4.81)	(1.12)
Random Coefficients[b,c]	-$60.10	-$65.76	-$37.47
	(4.16)	(3.01)	(1.09)
Closing of Northern Delaware Beaches			
Fixed Coefficients	-$160.43	-$171.15	-$195.27
	(12.92)	(7.31)	(2.62)
Random Coefficients[b,c]	-$117.20	-$120.56	-$106.58
	(8.01)	(4.93)	(2.52)
Lost Beach Width at All DE/MD/VA Developed Beaches			
Fixed Coefficients	-$57.68	-$54.44	-$77.78
	(14.18)	(16.14)	(6.29)
Random Coefficients[b,c]	-$35.51	-$35.30	-$33.91
	(8.71)	(9.58)	(3.82)

[a]Robust standard errors based on 200 Krinsky and Robb [1986] simulations in parentheses.

[b]The fixed coefficient Kuhn-Tucker welfare estimates were constructed with 25 simulations per observation. The random coefficient Kuhn-Tucker welfare estimates were constructed with 50 simulations per observation and a burn-in of 1000 simulations.

[c]The fixed coefficient Repeated Discrete Choice estimates were constructed with 2500 simulations. The random coefficient Repeated Discrete Choice estimates were constructed with 2500 simulations and a 1000 simulation burn-in.

Reviewer's Appendix Table: Repeated Discrete Choice Parameter Estimates

	Fixed Parameters	Random Parameters	
		Mean	Std. Dev.
Log-Likelihood	-27,869.91	-27,609.78	
Outside Alternative Dummy (OAD)	1.3704 (10.034)	-2.1745 (-5.422)	4.6603 (26.409)
OAD × ln(Age)	0.7735 (22.549)	2.1512 (18.686)	-
OAD × Kids under 10	0.1739 (8.759)	0.5076 (8.637)	-
OAD × Kids 10 to 16	-0.3350 (-17.338)	-0.9257 (-15.109)	-
OAD × Vacation Property in DE	-1.6901 (-53.823)	-1.5286 (-6.542)	9.6724 (19.905)
OAD × Retired	0.1529 (6.058)	0.5067 (6.645)	-
OAD × Student	-0.2757 (-9.107)	-0.8670 (-9.610)	-
Park	0.4551 (3.954)	0.1848 (1.531)	-
New Jersey Beach	-2.0416 (-25.906)	-12.243 (-11.343)	8.6077 (14.995)
Beach Length (Miles)	-0.1279 (-4.075)	0.1684 (5.291)	-
Boardwalk	0.2168 (1.942)	0.4474 (3.818)	-
Amusements	1.4503 (37.464)	0.9940 (21.000)	-
Private/Limited Access	-0.7885 (-16.027)	-0.8581 (-17.014)	-
Wide Beach	-0.8261 (-22.998)	-0.6614 (-20.138)	-
Narrow Beach	-0.6133 (-8.369)	-0.6030 (-7.898)	-
Atlantic City	1.8928 (18.165)	-4.4524 (-4.713)	6.2724 (9.740)
Surfing	0.8533 (23.715)	0.6530 (16.098)	-
High Rise	-0.1816 (-3.998)	-0.1895 (-4.065)	-
Park Within	1.9552 (18.312)	1.2072 (10.918)	-
Facility	-0.3691 (-5.757)	-0.2007 (-2.826)	-
Parking	0.9864 (7.844)	0.6295 (4.405)	-
MU of Income/100	2.9973 (71.531)	7.3238 (33.959)	-

t-statistics based on robust standard errors reported in parentheses
250 Halton draws used in estimation

MID-ATLANTIC REGION

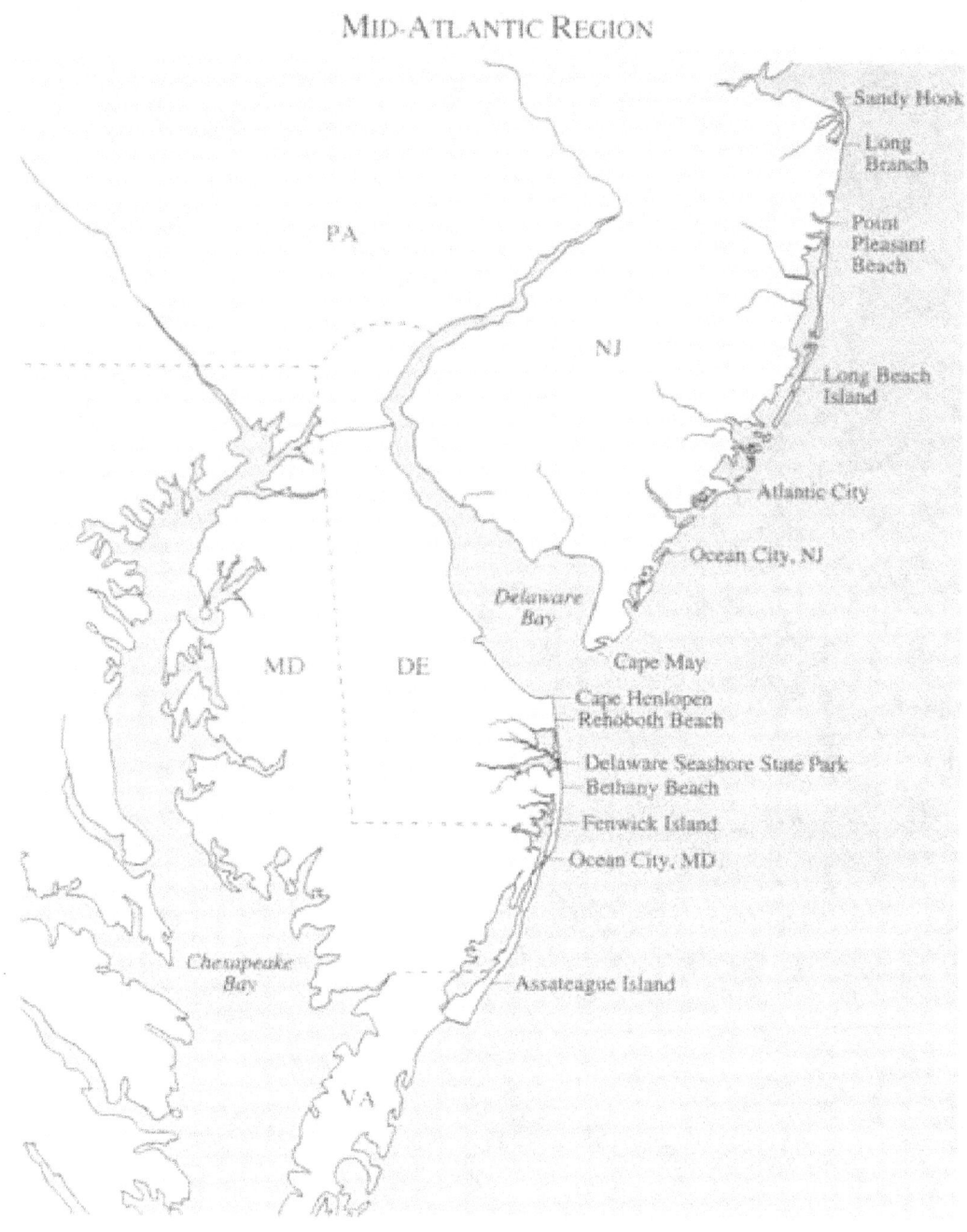

Figure 1: Map of Application Area